BELLWETHER MEDIA • MINNEAPOLIS, MN

Blastoff! Readers are carefully developed by literacy experts to build reading stamina and move students toward fluency by combining standards-based content with developmentally appropriate text.

Level 1 provides the most support through repetition of high-frequency words, light text, predictable sentence patterns, and strong visual support.

Level 2 offers early readers a bit more challenge through varied sentences, increased text load, and text-supportive special features.

Level 3 advances early-fluent readers toward fluency through increased text load, less reliance on photos, advancing concepts, longer sentences, and more complex special features.

★ **Blastoff! Universe**

This edition first published in 2021 by Bellwether Media, Inc.

Library of Congress Cataloging-in-Publication Data

Names: Moening, Kate, author.
Title: Delivery drivers / by Kate Moening.
Description: Minneapolis, MN : Bellwether Media, Inc., 2021. | Series:Blastoff! Readers: Community helpers | Includes bibliographical references and index. | Audience: Ages 5-8 | Audience: Grades K-1 | Summary: "Developed by literacy experts for students in kindergarten through grade three, this book introduces delivery drivers to young readers through leveled text and related photos"–Provided by publisher.
Identifiers: LCCN 2020029197(print) | LCCN 2020029198 (ebook) | ISBN 9781644874011 (Library Binding) | ISBN 9781648342417 (Paperback) | ISBN9781648340789 (ebook)
Subjects: LCSH: Professional motor vehicle drivers–Juvenile literature. | Delivery of goods–Juvenile literature.
Classification: LCC HF5761 .M68 2021 (print) | LCC HF5761 (ebook) | DDC388.4/132-dc23
LC record available at https://lccn.loc.gov/2020029197
LC ebook record available at https://lccn.loc.gov/2020029198

Editor: Betsy Rathburn Designer: Laura Sowers

Printed in the United States of America, North Mankato, MN.

Table of Contents

Special Delivery!

The delivery driver carries a **package** to the front door. Is anybody home?

package

The driver **scans** the box. He helps the **customer** sign for it. Next stop!

customer

What Are Delivery Drivers?

Delivery drivers carry packages. Some work for **shipment** companies.

Other drivers work for stores or **restaurants**. They bring people their **orders**!

What Do Delivery Drivers Do?

Delivery drivers load orders into trucks or vans. Some use their own cars.

Delivery Driver Gear
truck
map
scanner
cart

Delivery drivers load orders carefully. Carts help carry heavy packages.

cart

Drivers have many stops. They keep track of time. Do not be late!

What Makes a Good Delivery Driver?

Delivery drivers are good with people. They have many customers.

Delivery Driver Skills

- ✓ good with people
- ✓ strong
- ✓ good with maps
- ✓ good at driving

Delivery drivers are good with maps. They keep orders moving!

Glossary

customer

a person who pays for goods or services

restaurants

places where people can buy meals

orders

things that people buy or sell

scans

uses a special machine to copy information into a computer

package

a box or other package filled with things that have been mailed

shipment

related to companies that deliver goods for other businesses

To Learn More

AT THE LIBRARY

Leaf, Christina. *Mail Carriers.* Minneapolis, Minn.: Bellwether Media, 2018.

Rathburn, Betsy. *Truck Drivers.* Minneapolis, Minn.: Bellwether Media, 2020.

Sterling, Charlie W. *Where Does Mail Go?* Minneapolis, Minn.: Jump!, 2021.

ON THE WEB

FACTSURFER

Factsurfer.com gives you a safe, fun way to find more information.

1. Go to www.factsurfer.com.
2. Enter "delivery drivers" into the search box and click 🔍.
3. Select your book cover to see a list of related content.

Index

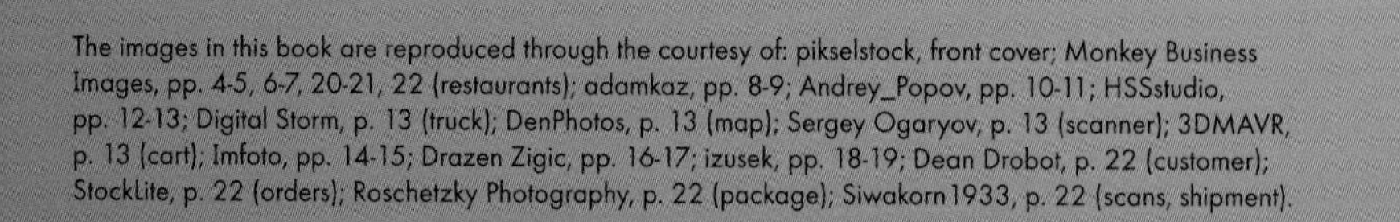

The images in this book are reproduced through the courtesy of: pikselstock, front cover; Monkey Business Images, pp. 4-5, 6-7, 20-21, 22 (restaurants); adamkaz, pp. 8-9; Andrey_Popov, pp. 10-11; HSSstudio, pp. 12-13; Digital Storm, p. 13 (truck); DenPhotos, p. 13 (map); Sergey Ogaryov, p. 13 (scanner); 3DMAVR, p. 13 (cart); Imfoto, pp. 14-15; Drazen Zigic, pp. 16-17; izusek, pp. 18-19; Dean Drobot, p. 22 (customer); StockLite, p. 22 (orders); Roschetzky Photography, p. 22 (package); Siwakorn1933, p. 22 (scans, shipment).